Mira's Blues

Poems By Jasmira

ISBN 979-8-9865579-0-8

Contents

TRUTH TO POWER

RANDOM WRITINGS/JUST TALKING

Dedication

This is dedicated to YOU. I give you my pain to sip slow, feel it, then let yours go.

Jasmira

"Live full, die empty." *Les Brown*

Self Love

More like a lack of

But Me

I saw an old friend he opened his arms, I stepped in.

I felt the want to in his embrace it felt nice, and I couldn't hide the smile it put on my face.

You can reach every goal to attain wealth untold, beyond measure or your wildest dreams.

No matter the amounts in your accounts; I'd rather have someone here to hear me scream.

Behind my smile, when I say

> I'm ok,

> Everything's cool

> I'm well and you

Some know it's all a screen.

No one's there when the dreams turn bad,

having me jump out my sleep to see, there is no one there... but me

There, I said it.

I hurt myself
There I said it
I cut myself but bled no blood.

Tears stained my pillow floor and bed
Pain hurt my head
So now I'm standing here embarrassed
No real job having real bills

Receiving hugs, I don't feel.

Everything is still numb
No, I'm not going to rhyme it with dumb.

Loving someone is never a mistake

It's knowing better and not doing better that
takes the cake

I hurt myself
There I said it.
I'm standing here in first gear moving at a
sloth's pace.
Trying to smile with tears streaming down my
face.

Are you ok?

I'm ok but my soul is crying out

It's looking for something it needs, it wants, it can't live without

It's punishing me for feeding it lies and deceit.

The pain hurts so bad that most nights I can't sleep

I don't toss and turn it's not comfort I seek

Nah, what's needed here, is way more deep.

It's a knowing that you're ok, you're alright, a whole person again

not some broken loser who can't find any way to win.

I miss something, I want it to call or come by.

I need it to hold me close

…Let me cry

A Break From

Feeling

Thinking

Eating

Responsibility

Heartbreak

Biting your tongue

The powers that be

Caring

Loving

Wanting

Needing

Heartache

Life…

You don't belong here

Sitting in a bar feeling out of place, looking around not recognizing one face. These people are strangers.

Shadows, reflections

Shouts, Screams

Whispers, Hope

Violent, Dreams

Scared, happy

Sad, joyous

Uncertain, unsure

Unhappy, frightened

So now what?

You don't belong here

Narrative for death is better than bondage & Win, When?

After I watched Black Panther, I wrote these two pieces. The strength, the power, the empowerment, the feeling of freedom, belonging, the prosperity This movie is everything.
Chadwick Boseman, you live on forever through your words and your movies.
Thank you.

Death Is Better Than Bondage

She said the baby cried all night.
The neighbors would say your baby is crying.
I know she'd say
Aren't you going to check on her?
I have
she's not hungry
not wet
doesn't want to be held
The doctors say it's not colic
She just cries.

She was 21, the baby a few months old,
Her 1-year-old, sound asleep amidst the
crying.

I say the baby took on the mother's pain
The hurt the sorrow the anger.
I say the baby didn't want to be born
I say the baby screamed for death.
Death is better than bondage.
There may not be chains the naked eye can see
But I'm not free
I'm haunted by what could have been

and will never be. My heart was broken in the womb
So much pain no words can my mouth speak
But my eyes these big, beautiful eyes
They tell on me.
I say I hide my sadness behind the scenes
but to my surprise others have seen it
My broken heart that is, for theirs was once broken too.
They tell me you are strong and this you will get through
Your pain will be exchanged for joy
beyond what you can imagine…
Just stay strong keep holding on
Meanwhile Kelly Price's song "Tired"
replays in my head
There's so much on me right now
I can't get out of bed
I keep looking for an escape, A way far away from me.
My dreams allow me a way out, for in my dreams I am free.

Win, When?

No one knows my struggle No one knows my
pain Some see my smile Some see it's
strained They know I'm a healer Those that
need help Where do I turn
When I need help myself
So many users So selfish & mean
Cause too many headaches Which leads to
disdain Got to keep pushing Got to speed it up
No time for excuses No 1 really cares
You're in this alone
Despite what some may say Some
things only you can deal with
Keep others BS at bay Long handled
spoons
1 in each hand That's one way to
deal
1 way to maintain control It's all about balance
And knowing when to let go
When to move on When to stop singing
sad songs
Writing sad pieces
Waiting for change
Seriously go make that happen
Practice discipline
You're worthy
I'll tell you that over & over again

Till you believe it Till you understand
You're a whole person
Smart, resilient & confident
You've survived through so much IT'S YOUR
TIME TO WIN.

Thinking Out Loud

I lied in my bed last night and I asked for snow
Sunday morning while sorting laundry, I
looked out the window to check the weather
and there was snow. I smiled big.

I wasn't ready to let winter go.

We talk about time moving fast.
We don't realize we are the reason.
Our words are rushing the seasons.
Global warming is a big factor as well.

But with our words we are casting spells.

We learned life and death are in the power of
the tongue.

Yet we speak as though we have none.

We feel what we say goes unheard.

Yet, our inner selves and the spiritual realm
heard every word.

We're casting spells and don't know it
We say things when in pain and despair.

When we're happy and when we don't care.

When things don't go our way, we're
wondering why
Not realizing our words live
They do not die.

We are always manifesting
Speaking to the universe, asking for blessings.

Not realizing we hold a power so true:

To change our own lives
And to change the world too.

Be cognizant of what you say
How you say it and to whom

Your very words can bring to your life
positivity and joy
Or gloom and doom

To Have and To Hold

I used to tell myself it would be nice to have
someone hold me.
 I should have said it would be nice to have the
person
assigned to me
To nurture me
Encourage me
Uplift me
Care about me
Take care of me
Protect me
Shield me
Speak life into me
Love me
Like me
Hold me.
 I wasn't specific
I settled for what was given.
accepted fake love and all that comes with it.

Now if asked what I want. I can say with
certainty
I want freedom from living in fear. I want the
keys to the prison I've built, I'm not happy
here.
 I'm not safe.

not protected at all.
More than my heart will break, if I continue to fall.

I say this now
loud and clear
That I no longer live in fear.

I live in light
I live in truth
I live in love
I live in you
I live in me
I am free from what once had me bound.
I have all the riches
And yes, the glory too

I've been given authority
To conquer all enemies

I am resilient
I have the strength
and power
to reach all heights
I use my resources and a little might.
I tell myself yes.
I no longer say no
It's up to me
how far I go

I can stand still
Or be a leaf
Riding the wind
I'm a forever friend
Which is a good friend indeed.
    I live in happiness
    I live in peace
    I live in faith
Negativity, I ceased
    I live in God
    God lives in me
Every second
A blessing
Every minute a gift
You too can live a life like this.
Do something new
 set new goals.
This life is yours to have and hold.

Make up your mind to start right now, to love
yourself; not be a clown
A fool for love is a fool for pain
While you lose
And they continue to gain
If you need help
Just ask,
 it's there
Your guardian is always with you.

And yes, they care.
You're told you entered this world alone
but that's not true.
You can always phone home.

Make up your mind
Decide every minute
That with every breath
You're going to win it.

Win what you may ask
Well, that's up to you
You know what you want and what you must
do.

Just know, I love you
No matter where I am.
I send you strength
Love, light, faith, and peace.
Continue to Speak what you seek
Even after you see what you said
Be intentional with your words, as there's
power in the tongue. You're the one who
decides if you lose or if you've won. Keep
pressing on the upward way.
Every day you awaken is yours for the taking.
Age is truly a number.
Don't focus to much on it

It will stress you out and delay your goals

Remember: this life is yours, *to have and hold.*

Notes: _____

_____

_____

_____

_____

_____

_____

_____

_____

_____

_____

_____

_____

_____

_____

_____

_____

_____

_____

TRUTH TO POWER

Workplace Musings

We view the world through different lenses
your Vision's clear

mine is blended

some say the world is black and white

it's not that simple

this gift of sight

you wake up

go through life

don't see the pain, don't see the strife

everything was made for you

the fairy tale you created
this land you stole
And decimated

The lies you told and continue to tell
If I had it my way

you would know the hell You

put my people through.

Yeah, my vengeance would be slow and methodical

See my thinking diabolical

I'd make you feel every bit of the pain you caused my people

My words lethal

Have you praying for the mercy you didn't give us?

Yet you say "In God we trust"

"Jesus loves you oh dear slave, your reward is coming after you're in your grave"

So, pray to your Jesus, that he set you free
But there will be no mercy granted to you from me.

By Whatever Means

NO JUSTICE
         NO PEACE

Still marching
         these streets

                  Hurt,
                  tired
                  Beaten,
                  broken

You may have killed the dreamer
The militant speaker
But truth crushed to earth will rise again

BLACK POWER

         NO JUSTICE

                  NO PEACE

                           STOP RACIST ENTITIES

                                    By Whatever Means

Fresh off my mind: Part 1

All cops aren't bad, it's only a few.

Some will argue, not to do what they do.

To that I say fuck you.

We're done being subdued.
Told to stifle, like Archie told Edith

While our people are shot dead in the street...
bleeding.

Or at Wal-Mart, wherever cops are called

While we're shopping, or chilling at the mall

While we're playing catch in our yards,

driving around the city in souped up cars.

Hearts broken

faces wet from tears we're crying

As another of us lies there dying.

We're not taking anymore
racism, discrimination, all the pain endured.

Sat in,
    held marches,
            hosed down,
                    turned the other cheek

As lynched bodies hanged from the poplar
trees.

Kneeled, even begged for our lives
Stilled killed
 left with twisted mouths & bulging eyes,

Blood everywhere
            Nobody cares
As long as we are dead, they can still live their
lie.

Part 2

Terrorists, murderers, you call them police.
All I know is what I see, all that's happening to
people who look like me.
And what I believe and see is that

I CAN'T BREATHE!

I'm losing my breath!

My heart is pounding

Beating so fast inside

my chest!

I want retribution
Revenge of some kind

But the God served by many

Says vengeance is mine

Where are you God?
Why are you letting this be?
Just like in the days of slavery
Where were you then?
All the singing and praying
Could you not hear the cries and the pleas?
Asking for freedom, to live and just be.
With no feet on our necks; *definitely,* no knees
With our last breath saying, pleading,
we can't breathe.

My heart broken while they're choking the life out of us. What recourse do we have, marching and protests?
There must be more that can be done. No matter who is in office, they're still killing us one by one.

Part 3

We've turned the other cheek
We've marched to the beat
We took up Christianity
We've endured blistered feet
We've held our children in our arms
As they lay dying in the streets

Where are the Nat Turners?
The Harriet Tubmans?

We've asked why us
We've prayed to their God
We believed one day
We'd be free
Alive but not living
We can't allow this to be
To continue.
From 1619 to 2019 to today
we've endured too much to say.

Friday Night Writings

Beat us
Bruised us
Cooked us
Used us
Digested us
Confused us
Signed for us
Never. Cosigned for us

Transported
Sorted

THESE ONES TOBACCO.
         THIS GROUP RICE
THOSE OVER THERE COTTON…
                  enslaved for life.

Auctioned, SOLD

Equal to cattle
Priced less than gold… not one lie told

Hung us innocent
The guilty went free
Emmett Till gone would be in his 80s now.
His killer still free.

She kissed her husband in court, smiled proud and big.
To them they slaughtered an animal, not a 14-year-old kid.

Billy sang "Southern trees bear strange fruit, blood on the leaves and blood at the roots"

Held picnics
Where you picked niggers to hang

Brought children to see
Now you all fight to end any teachings of slavery… Wait, my bad, y'all call it critical race theory.

Even call us racist now, while weaponizing your hate
You're the victims now?
Y'all had human zoos

Guess who was in the cage?

And now WE'RE the ones with all the rage?

Well DAMN, we should be angry, we've earned every right to be.
Despite what you do to erase your past.

My ancestors are alive; they LIVE and tell their story through me.

Notes:

_____

_____

_____

_____

_____

_____

_____

_____

_____

_____

_____

_____

Just take it

When they hit us, kick us, not promote us, kill us, degrade us, berate us, dehumanize us, we're told to just take it.

Why are we treated like we deserve the behavior they exhibit towards us?

Like anything horrible, they've ever done to us i.e., our enslavement and everything that followed was our fault.

Management can say and do what they want, we attempt to a resolution they dig in and continue to attack. Others ask you "What can we do, instead of addressing the problem.

We are supposed to Just Take It.

Notes:

Until Everyone Dies

I want to do something, maybe scream, or
shout. I must find a way to get it all out. See,
I'm so angry, but I'll do what's best for me and
allow my words to speak:

I know collectively we can't allow this to be.
A country divided
Hate and change are words you hear most.
There are people dying, crying, asking
why and
            people being accused of being violent

            Being blamed for our own deaths

All the while we're all on the ground losing our
breaths.

You may see one handcuffed dying at the
hands or by the knees of police
But we see millions all the way back to the
times of slavery. You saw a murder of 1 and
said enough was enough, thank you for the
marching and protesting with us. But until it's
everyone united as one; it'll continue to be
                just us...

---

dying senselessly, for reasons you won't
believe.

You could ask,
            we could explain
but your privilege conceives what we say as
excuses.

To continue to be useless and deserving to die
because our skin doesn't matter.
It's ingrained in you that darker hue is badder,
unless it's your tan
by which you're flattered.

My skin tans in the sun too but when winter
comes, I'll still be of a darker hue, Still dealing
with injustices as equality is not for us

You'll shake your head
saying; what a shame,
Who's to blame?
This continues to happen to
them.
Never realizing it's
happening to us all.

The bible says "see your neighbor as yourself"
your neighbors aren't just the people who live

next door. Your neighbors are the people you
see in the world.

Maybe your view of you is askew. Which
makes it difficult to view others as you.

To see me die in an unnatural way and to shake
your head
While you walk away
Says too much about this country
 and it's humanity.

How can fellow humans allow this to be?
Days after weeks, months after years
No care, no concern for the dying, the dead; no
tears.

No attempts to stop it, even on the smallest
scale

Maybe you feel powerless or are scared of
being, criticized, ostracized.

Maybe you're a coward, or you just don't care,
it's not happening to anyone you know

so, you don't get involved, and it continues to
continue, and it evolves.

Like a virus, fighting to stay alive, mutating, getting stronger until everyone dies.

[Remaining ignorant leads to your own demise.]

Notes:

_____

_____

_____

_____

_____

_____

_____

_____

_____

_____

_____

_____

_____

Just Talking

Narrative for Did You?

Chatting with a friend about people who show up at your funeral. When they wanted nothing to do with you in life. I say, treat me the way you did the day before you learned I died. Keep that same energy! Bitch

Did You?

Did you show your loved one love while they were living?
Did you pick up the phone and call?
Did you make amends for any hurt that you caused?

Did you attempt to right any wrongs?
While you cry trying to sing these sad songs?
As you remember the fun times you had.

All the times they made you laugh.

You smile through the tears at the memory

But did you ever tell them you loved them, made sure they could see.

That they weren't just words you were saying, you really cared, and gave a damn

Or did you let the pain take precedence remained silent, maintained distance.

So, you showed up here to what? Pay respect, hoping somehow, they will know and forgive you.

Keep it a stack, Keep it 100

Don't sit up in here pretending
y'all were down. Ace boon coons;
riding for each other... straight goons

Nah be as honest as you were when they were living.

Get on with the bullshit you're not forgiven.

Uncrowned King

Pt1.

In these streets I'd rather see you posed with a book than a bottle.

Who cares what brand of alcohol you like; it all burns when you swallow?

You drive past memorials all you see is empty bottles and teddy bears.

Is that how you want to be remembered, empty bottles and teddy bears?

All it says to me is your life was going nowhere.

You died in the streets most likely under the age of 25

Leaving your loved ones to mourn and say goodbye.

Pt2.

Your life matters

Do something

Drinking and getting high

Unemployed Carrying guns

Living a life that yields nothing

But hey you're having fun

Your life matters

If it didn't, we'd still be slaves

No one would have fought for change

Martin and all the others would not have been slain

Fighting for rights you now throw away

Walking through your life but stuck in the same day,

Your life matters

but you're living it on repeat

Pants hanging off your behind

Sleeping all day, at night running the streets

 Your life matters

yet you're doing nothing to progress

Selling drugs, thinking you're a thug; young man you are not hopeless

Your sisters need you those who share your blood and those who don't

Stop expecting someone else to step up trust me; they won't.

Your life matters despite the environment you may be in…. None of us can do it alone

We must work together to win….

Pt.3

Your life gone, sad songs

They will sing.

Your mom, oh your mom

Can't stop crying

Remembering your birth

While coming to grips with your dying

So many questions unanswered

Her heart barely beating

Asking why God, did you really need him?

Her baby is gone

She feels she's dreaming

When she's able to sleep

She wakes up screaming

Why him lord?

Did you really need him?

He had so many plans

His life was just beginning

Now she has to say goodbye

While feeling like her life is ending

Uncrowned King

Though I didn't know you.

Your life is gone.

You won't get to show who

You really what you can do

The plans you had to make it through

 Uncrowned King

Those who knew you are preparing to say goodbye

Through it asking why did you have to die?

Why were you there?

What were you doing?

So many unanswered questions another life ruined.

Not finished

Are they pieces or ammunition?
Is it therapy helping me to get out my feelings?
Maybe it's a form of release helping me to
exhale
Keep my nerves calm, allowing me not to dwell
On should of, could of and would of or is the
correct word not of, but have?

Maybe it's not ammunition may be its fuel for
the fire
That will spark the flame
That will allow others to rise higher
Not accept defeat
And the weight of others
Not carry the burden put on them by their
mothers

Notes:
_____
_____
_____
_____
_____
_____
_____

The Cigarette

Always having to get up

When that need arises

When that want starts to call

Wishing you never started such a habit

wishing you could let if fall

By the wayside.

Unable to hide

From the damage it's causing

To your body and your wallet

When that need is strong

You can't think can't focus

Asked what's up,

Your unable to call it

All you can think about is feeding that habit

Out in the cold

Getting whipped by the wind

Sweating under the heat of the sun

Unable to turn back

Unable to run

Unable to quit

spending your last dime just to get that next hit

the feel of the cigarette between your fingers

taking that first puff allowing the smoke to
linger

giving no regard to all that you could do and
have
imagine if you will the money you would save
if to the cigarette you weren't a slave.

We As Black People

I don't put famous people or celebrities as they are called higher than myself. Sure, I've met a few but we as black people are celebrities as well. Gods and Goddesses, if you will.

People get surgeries to have what we were born with.
But they can't surgically implant our spirit.

Heaven And Earth

You move heaven and earth
    for things to get worse
You walk around
    as if you're on shaky ground.
You have days when you're okay
    And days you want everyone to go away

In case you were wondering

I meant every word, the ones spoken and
silently heard,

We hear all the time how time is of the essence,
to wake up every day is more than a blessing.

It's an opportunity,
a chance to do something huge.
Something that makes a positive difference
not a chance you should abuse.

I find I talk a lot more than I care to,
I guess in my own way I'm scared not to,
I'm trying to leave it all here.
I want to leave this world empty.
Just wanted to share this... in case you were
wondering

Notes:

www.ingramcontent.com/pod-product-compliance
Lightning Source LLC
Chambersburg PA
CBHW070029110426
42741CB00034B/2695